ANIMAL
families

A Two Hands Production Ltd production
as seen on Channel Five

Dorling Kindersley

I love hide-and-seek. Mummy will never find me up here!

LONDON, NEW YORK, MELBOURNE, MUNICH, and DELHI

Written and edited by Lorrie Mack
Project Designer Gemma Fletcher

Designers Mary Sandberg, Sonia Moore
Editors Penny Arlon, Alexander Cox, Penny Smith

Consultant Kim Dennis-Bryan PhD. FZS

Publishing Manager Bridget Giles
Managing Art Editor Rachael Foster
Category Publisher Mary Ling

Production Controller Claire Pearson
Production Editor Clare McLean
Jacket Editor Mariza O'Keefe

First published in Great Britain in 2008 by
Dorling Kindersley Limited,
80 Strand, London, WC2R 0RL

ISBN 978-1-40533-250-7

Colour reproduction by Alta Image, UK
Printed in Singapore by Star Standard Pte Ltd

Discover more at
www.dk.com

contents

Wait up! Walking isn't easy with little legs. I hope we stop and rest soon.

just like us

Do you live, learn, eat, and play with your family? Animals do too!

We are animals, just like elephants, monkeys, lions, bears, and hippos are animals. Like your parents, many animal parents take care of their children and make sure they're safe.

Which of our animal families

Learning new skills and tricks is an important part of growing up.

Your mum and dad make sure you have the right foods to eat.

Animal parents often cuddle their babies too, and play with them, and even make sure their faces and their fur are neat. About the only thing they don't do is nag about homework!

reminds you of your own?

animal families

Mums and dads together or apart, one child or lots of children, close friends or groups of relations – they're all families!

Cattle live in big groups called herds. Within one herd, many of the calves might be related. They all play, rest, and eat together.

rooster

I live with my children and their mum, and I like to make sure they all behave themselves!

hen

The people we live with are called our

More's a crowd

Do you ever go out with your friends' family? These young hippos are being looked after by two mums.

There are lots of different human families too. Some have one parent, some have two, and some have aunts, uncles, and grandparents as well.

He's the boss

Giraffe herds are often led by one or two strong males. All the females and children follow them.

family.

family facts

There are all sorts of animal families with different ways of life. Here are a few:

Raccoon mums raise their children alone. They leave them in the safest place they can find, like this cosy log.

Dad's turn

If you were a seahorse dad, you would carry eggs in a safe pouch on your body until they're ready to hatch as baby seahorses.

What's life like in your family?

A male sea
lion is called
a bull. He has
lots of wives.
After mating,
he will go off
and live alone.

Left alone

After a baby sea lion is born
(this one is *brand* new), his
mum takes care of him for
only a few days before she
needs to go off to find food.

Turn and turn about

Baby penguins are looked after
all the time. Their parents
leave to find food as well, but
they take turns looking after
their little one.

9

new babies

A baby is about the most exciting thing that can arrive in a family. Newborns are very small and weak, so their mums have to take extra-special care of them.

cow and calf

All worn out
This tired mother lynx cuddles her new baby close and shuts her eyes.

Seven or eight baby blue-tits usually hatch at one time, so their mum and dad have lots of hungry new babies to look after.

orang-utans

mum's milk

When they're first born, lots of baby animals live on milk they get from their mummy. Later, babies grow big enough to eat grown-up food.

People drink milk from their mummy too. Some babies keep on doing this even after they've started eating solid food.

Jacob sheep

Puma cubs are born blind and deaf, so it's a good thing they don't have to look far for food.

Mothers' milk is best

Liquid lunch

Babies drink milk from their mum's breasts. This hungry little sea cow (sometimes called a *manatee*) can even do it under water!

My brothers and sisters and I are all VERY hungry. Because mum sometimes has three babies, she has several breasts, or teats. I just hope there's enough milk!

grizzly bears

for babies – it makes them strong.

brothers and sisters

How many brothers and sisters do you have? Animals often have lots and lots, and sometimes they are all born at the same time!

Kittens love playing with their family. Three to five are normally born together.

These little piggies...

... live in a big family. Their mums usually have up to ten babies, or even more.

Getting into mischief is so much

Sheep are a bit like people – they tend to have just one baby, or twins.

Puppy love

Big dogs like labradors can have up to 14 puppies at a time. What a lot of puppies!

Full load

How many of her babies can this mother goosander fit on her back?

more fun when there's a gang of us.

out for the day

Mum likes us all to go exploring together.

swan and cygnets

We can walk and swim as soon as we hatch out of our eggs. We like to waddle down to the pond with our mum, but I can't always keep up with the other ducks.

Sometimes my brother bumps into
me (he says it's an accident but
I'm not sure). It's OK, though – if
I trip over, someone's always there
to make sure I'm all right.

quack
quack!

home sweet home

tortoises

Houses keep humans safe and warm, and many animals build shelters too. One animal – the tortoise – even carries his house around with him on his back. It's called a shell.

rabbit

After bouncing around, I like to go to sleep in my cosy underground tunnels, called a warren.

Some animals live underground –

Tree houses

Lots of birds build nests in hollow trees to keep their chicks safe. Using their beaks, the birds make soft beds out of twigs, leaves, moss, and anything else they can find.

Each night I make myself a nest from leaves and branches high in the treetops. I hope I don't fall out!

orang-utan

some live high up in the trees.

rise and shine

It's hard to get moving in the mornings when you feel warm and sleepy. Sometimes baby animals have trouble waking up too.

Baby red foxes (called cubs) wake up in the safety of a sheltered den.

zebra

These playful polar bears are making sure their mum doesn't sleep in.

Sniff sniff! The morning air smells funny.

Even for a wild rabbit, there's nothing like a good yawn and a stretch to start the day.

gorillas

welcome to the world

Animal mummies kiss and nuzzle their babies to make sure they feel close and safe. This process, which is called "bonding", continues all through childhood.

cheetahs

If a new mum doesn't bond with her

Safe smell

After two or three days, a baby zebra (called a foal) knows its mum by her smell, her voice, and the way she looks. Until then, mum won't let any other member of the herd near.

I get to know my mum by rubbing her furry face with my nose and licking it with my tongue.

Brrrrrr

This tiny seal has just been born on the ice in Antarctica. Its mum will soon leave to find food. When she gets back, she'll find her baby by its smell.

baby, she may not take care of it.

rabbit

neat and tidy

Sometimes your mum helps you wash your face and hands and brush your hair, and sometimes you do these things yourself. Animals like to be well groomed too.

A mother red deer licks her baby, called a fawn. This licking comforts him and keeps him neat.

Wash time
This baby lemur has both his mum and his aunt to look after him. A quick lick and his face is nice and clean.

kittens

Cats not only groom themselves, they also groom each other. If your kitten licks you, it means he likes and trusts you.

Baboons spend lots of time checking each other's fur. Tiny insects crawl in it and cause itching, so it's good to have a friend to help dig them out.

Why don't children *ever* clean their ears?

25

taking a dip

There's nothing elephants enjoy more than messing around in water holes. Once they get in, they don't ever want to get out again!

When they're little, human babies can't control their arms and legs very well. In the same way, a baby elephant's trunk is a bit floppy at first.

Elephants splash in water to keep clean, to cool down, and to get rid of the tiny bugs that live on their skin.

Baby elephants REALLY LOVE

I can suck up lots of water in my trunk, then curl it around and treat myself to a nice shower.

to play in muddy water.

feeding chicks

mealtime

Your mum might give you meat or rice for your meals, but animal children can feed on grass, or nuts, or bugs. Birds even pop worms into their babys' beaks.

Family grazing
These rhinos eat mostly grasses. Like cattle, they wander over the land, snacking as they go.

Lots of creatures, and especially big cats, eat other animals. When lion cubs play roughly together, they're learning how to hunt and kill.

If I can just get this nut open, we can have what's inside for our supper.

eat your greens

Some animals, like some humans, eat only plants – no fish or meat. The trouble with eating just vegetation is that you have to eat a huge amount to give you all the energy you need.

koala

Reach for the grub
Giraffes have *long, long* necks so they can chew the highest branches where no other animal can reach.

Seeds, nuts, and vegetables are scrumptious! Do you think you could be a vegetarian too?

This forest is the perfect place to pick up a snack.

mountain gorilla

gone fishing

Yum, yum – fish for supper! Do your parents buy fish from a shop and cook it for you? If young animals want fish to eat, they have to learn to catch it all by themselves.

Otters catch and eat lots and lots of fish. This mum shows her pup how it's done.

Watch and learn

Baby seals learn to catch fish when they're a few weeks old, but they can swim almost as soon as they're born. Their special mum's milk puts on a thick layer of fat to keep them warm in water.

Fish is just as good for you as it is for baby animals – it makes your bones strong and strengthens your eyes, brain, and heart too.

Fresh fish is very fast food –

Keep watching the water – when a nice, fat salmon swims by, grab it! The hard part is standing on the slippery rocks without falling in.

grizzly bears

and it's really healthy, too!

carry me mum

When you were very small, your mum and dad carried you around. Animal parents carry their babies too – on their back, in a pouch, or even in their teeth!

I cling to mum's back, even when she climbs eucalyptus trees to pick leaves for supper.

koalas

Little legs aren't as strong as big

A tiny wallaby stays in its mum's pouch all the time. Even older babies like to snuggle inside when they get tired of jumping.

When human children sit on grown-ups' shoulders, we say they're having a piggyback, but pigs don't do this!

Precious package

When they're babies, all cats – from lions to family pets – get carried in their mum's teeth. She holds the skin on their neck very, very gently.

Baby gorillas can't walk far until they're about nine months old. Until then, they hang on to their mum's fur and ride on her back.

ones – sometimes they need help.

hide and seek

Certain animals are very hard to see, because they blend in with their surroundings. Sometimes their disguise protects them from enemies, and sometimes it helps them hide so they can attack other animals.

plover

plover eggs on rocky shore

A covering that makes something

Double duty

Since his fluffy baby coat looks like grass, this young cheetah can hide from his enemies. When he grows up, he'll hide from animals he's hunting so he can pounce.

Nobody will find us here – we can nibble all this tasty grass in peace.

mountain goats

hard to see is called *camouflage.*

mummy and me

Hippopotamuses love the water – their closest living relatives are whales and porpoises. A hippo mum usually has just one baby at a time, and she keeps a very close eye on it for the first year of its life.

Hippos are so heavy, they can walk along the bottom of lakes and rivers. They take their time, since adults can hold their breath for about five minutes.

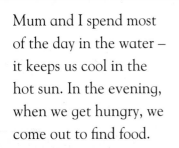

Mum and I spend most of the day in the water – it keeps us cool in the hot sun. In the evening, when we get hungry, we come out to find food.

There are lots of other animals in the river and on the shore, but I always feel safe with my mum close by. She shows me where to go and protects me from danger.

playtime

orang-utan

What's your favourite time of day? Playtime of course! Animal babies love to play too – it's an important part of learning and growing up.

Mummy! Look at me! I can stand on my own two feet. Do I look like a big grizzly bear yet?

Play is fun! It helps you learn,

Chimpanzee trampoline

Ready or not, here I come! This chimpanzee mum plays with her baby to show her love. Do you play with your mummy?

Some play looks painful, but it's mostly for show. A good scrap helps babies learn how to hunt prey and survive in the wild.

kittens

Slip, slide, and glide

Emperor penguins never have to wish for snow! They have fun sliding on ice at the south pole!

keep fit, and make friends.

climbing trees

Do you like climbing trees? Some animals live in trees, play in trees, and find all their food in trees too.

brown bear

Scrambling up branches makes my muscles strong. When I grow up, I'll be too big to climb so high!

raccoons

This porcupine mum and baby climb trees to eat leaves and bark. If they eat too much, the tree will die.

Playing in trees is good exercise –

In the tree tops

Hairy three-toed sloths spend almost all their lives hanging around in trees. They only come down once a week to leave droppings.

I don't like to move too fast. As long as I visit a tree or two day, I'm happy.

as long as you don't fall out!

43

using tools

In the same way that you use a spoon or a fork to pick up your food, chimpanzees use sticks to collect the insects they find so delicious.

I'm sure there are lots more fat juicy ants in here.

Only the smartest animals are

Chimps sometimes chew the end of a stick so it fits better into the holes of an ant colony or termite nest.

Captive supper
For easy access to tempting termites, it's a good idea to sit right on top of their nest.

Apart from humans, only a few other animals use tools. Apes, monkeys, sea otters, and some birds use tools.

able to find and adapt tools.

sending signals

Mummy where are you? Babies and parents talk to each other in many ways. A lost penguin chick recognizes its mother's voice from thousands of others. But baby-talk isn't just about sound...

penguin

Barking orders
Seal mums grunt and touch to show love and protect their newborn babies.

Parents use signals to comfort,

bottle-nose dolphin

Clickety-click. Listen to my songs and clicks and follow along.

meerkats

Look out

Playtime is safe with meerkat dad keeping watch. His children can tell just by the way he stands and looks that he's watching over them.

protect, and teach their babies.

watch me wobble

Almost all grass-eating animals – like horses and zebras – have to stand up on their feet in the first hour after they're born. No wonder they're a bit wobbly!

It's hard to keep your balance when your legs are so long and thin!

Baby wildebeests need a lot of get up and go – their herds are always on the move, so they have to run about 20 minutes after they're born.

follow my leader

When groups of animals move from place to place, one adult usually leads the way. Babies and children follow along behind...

Baby polar bears stay with mum when she goes off to find food. This outing is probably their first – and their mum's first – since they were born.

penguin chicks

This way everybody!

The matriarch is the female elephant in charge of a herd. She takes the lead when the whole herd moves off to find water.

I've got all these chicks to look after – I hope nobody gets lost!

proud parents

lion cub

Lions are the rulers of the jungle – fierce hunters that all the other animals are afraid of. When it comes to their children, though, mummy and daddy lions are big pussycats.

Hello mum

When it's bonding with its mother, a baby lion crawls all over her, and enjoys a bit of friendly pushing and shoving too.

Sometimes human babies hurt their parents when they don't mean to, by scratching, or biting, or poking.

Loving parents often allow

CAREFUL – that's not stroking, that's scratching – and it hurts!

a bit of naughtiness.

I need a hug

When you're tired, or sad, or frightened, a hug is the very nicest thing. Animals comfort their families too – in whatever way suits them best.

These ring-tailed lemurs all want a hug from mum at the same time.

There, there
Elephants can't hug each other like we can, but an older sister's reassuring trunk has the same effect.

A comforting cuddle always

Japanese macaques

I'll look after my children for years after they're born, and keep in touch with them for the rest of my life.

makes you feel better.

staying safe

All through the animal kingdom, mothers and fathers
do everything they can to keep their children safe.
Their protection can take many different forms.

Eyes focussed

Meerkat families search for food in the warm sunshine.
Here, the little ones scour the ground in search of insects,
while the grown-ups keep a protective watch.

polar bears

When I feel scared, I try to hide behind my mum's big, furry body.

If there is danger, shaggy muskoxen make a circle around their young. These parents are just moving into place.

time for bed

dormouse

Some baby animals sleep at night, some during the day. Some sleep in nests, some in trees – and some just find a nice bit of ground.

We like to sleep during the day, when the sun is hot. During the cool night, we look for food.

ZZZZZZZZZZZZZZZZZ

In the tree tops

Squirrel monkeys not only spend all day in the trees, they sleep there too. They have a special instinct, or sense, that stops them from falling off.

Animals that are active during the day and sleep at night (like you and me) are called *diurnal.* The ones that sleep during the day are called *nocturnal.*

Baby owls (called owlets) sleep in trees too. These brothers and sisters snuggle together on a safe branch.

ZZZZZZZZZZZZZZZZZZZZZzzzzzzzz..............

the end

Now you've seen how lots of animals live with their families. Which baby animal did you like best?

gorilla

Please come and

We're all off to find new feeding places, play in cool rivers and lakes, and explore the countryside!

visit us again soon.

glossary

What does it all mean? Here are the meanings of some words that will help you learn about animal families.

bonding when a parent and baby take time to know and love each other.

breasts the area of an animal that produces milk.

brood a collection of young animals cared for at one time.

colony a group of animals (like penguins) that live closely together.

diurnal an animal that is awake during the day and sleeps at night.

herd a large group of animals that travels together.

instinct natural feeling animals have from birth (rather than something they learn), which helps them survive.

mammal an animal with fur that drinks its mother's milk when it's a baby.

mating when a male and female come together to produce babies.

matriarch the female in charge of a group of animals.

nocturnal an animal that is awake at night and sleeps during the day.

prey an animal that is hunted for food.

relatives members of a family, like brothers and sisters, uncles, and aunts.

teat the nipple of a female where a baby drinks milk.

The bigger you grow, the

picture credits

The publisher would like to thank the following for their kind permission to reproduce their photographs:

(Key: a-above; b-below/bottom; c-centre; l-left; r-right; t-top): **Alamy Images:** Arco Images 14tl; Steve Austin/ Papilio 9bl; Blickwinkel/ Kaufung 24cl; Blickwinkel/ Weber 6tr; Andrew Fox 29bc, bl, br; Jonathan Hewitt 26c; Juniors Bildarchiv 6b; Erich Kuchling/ Westend 61 15c; Thomas D Mangelsen/ Peter Arnold, Inc. 33; Martin Phelps 14c; Photo Network/ Bill Bachmann 4bl; Steve Bloom Images 7tc, 28bc, br; Duncan Usher 21br, 24tl; Brent Ward 7br; WorldFoto 46tr. **Ardea:** Uno Berggren 19tr; Elizabeth Bomford 32cl; John Daniels 54tl; Jagdeep Rajput 60-61. **Corbis:** O. Alamany & E. Vicens 11t; Tom Brakefield 55; W. Perry Conway 10c; George McCarthy 11br; Joe McDonald 28cr; Paul Souders 22tl, 27; Gabriela Staebler/ Zefa 23tr; Kennan Ward 57br. **DK Images:** Barleylands Farm Museum and Animal Centre, Billericay 15cla; Two Hand Promotions 7cl, 22-23, 30crb, 37tl, 38bc, br, 39bc, bl, br, 52c, 53, 56c, 59t. **Michael Fiddleman 2008:** 9tl. **FLPA:** Tui De Roy/ Minden Pictures 18tl; Tim Fitzharris/ Minden Pictures 42cr; Michael & Patricia Fogden/ Minden Pictures 43; Sumio Harada/ Minden Pictures 37b; Mitsuaki Iwago/ Minden Pictures 34; Frans Lanting 1, 32cr; Yva Momatiuk & John Eastcott/ Minden Pictures 40b; Pete Oxford/ Minden Pictures 29t; Fritz Polking 31; Ingo Schulz/ Imagebroker 35tl; Jurgen & Christine Sohns 46c; Sunset 41cr; Tom Vezo/ Minden Pictures 36cla; Michael Weber/ Imagebroker 47r; Konrad Wothe/ Minden Pictures 36b, 42br, cl; Norbert Wu/ Minden Pictures 23cr. **Getty Images:** James Balog 44-45; The Image Bank/ Andy Rouse 52tr; The Image Bank/ Daniel J. Cox 8cr; The Image Bank/ Joseph Van Os 50-51; Beverly Joubert/ National Geographic 38-39t; Jochen Luebke/ AFP 38cl; Michael Melford 54b; Minden Pictures/ Norbert Wu 8bl; Minden Pictures/ ZSSD 60tl; Photographer's Choice/ Daniel J Cox 20cra; Photographer's Choice/ Johan Elzenga 5br; Photographer's Choice RR/ Ronald Wittek 8tl; Reportage/ Paula Bronstein 2; Riser/ Darrell Gulin 25; Robert Harding World Imagery/ Thorsten Milse 21tr, 50cra; Science Faction/ Konrad Wothe 9tr; Manoj Shah 45tr; Stone - Daniel J Cox 56-57; Stone/ Anup Shah 58c; Stone/ David Trood 4-5t; Stone/ Jose Luis Pelaez 5cr; Taxi/ Benelux Press 28tl; Taxi/ Stan Osolinski 51tl. **iStockphoto.com:** Debra McGuire 47. **naturepl.com:** Eric Baccega 3, 13b; Bernard Castelein 59cr; Todd Pusser 13tr; Gabriel Rojo 12cr; Anup Shah 12tl, 40tl, 41tr, 48bc, br, cl, 49bc, bl, br; Shattil & Rozinski 63; Carol Walker 48-49; Wegner/ Arco 35cr. **NHPA/ Photoshot:** Stephen Dalton 58tl. **Photolibrary:** OSF/ Rob Nunnington 20-21; OSF/ Mike Powles 24cr. **PunchStock:** Digital Vision 10tr, 16-17; Photodisc/ John Giustina 5tr. **Still Pictures:** Compost/ Visage 19b. **SuperStock:** Age Fotostock 16clb; ZSSD 30tl.

Jacket images: Front: **Getty Images:** Robert Harding World Imagery/ Thorsten Milse. Back: **Alamy Images:** Steve Bloom Images c; **Corbis:** Paul Souders cl.

All other images © Dorling Kindersley
For further information see: www.dkimages.com

deer

bigger the words you know.

63

index

DK would like to thank Rob Nunn, Julia Harris-Voss and Natalie Godwin for help with this book.